# THE PAST
# DOESN'T HAVE
# A FUTURE,
# BUT YOU DO

# THE PAST DOESN'T HAVE A FUTURE, BUT YOU DO

### ACHIEVING THE FUTURE THAT'S IN YOUR HANDS

## BYRD BAGGETT

CUMBERLAND HOUSE

Published by Cumberland House Publishing, Inc.

Cover design: Gore Studio, Inc.
Text design: Lisa Taylor

Library of Congress Cataloging-in-Publication Data

Baggett, Byrd.
 The past doesn't have a future, but you do : achieving the future that's in your hands / Byrd Baggett.
  p.  cm.
ISBN 978-1-58182-364-6  (pbk.)
ISBN 978-1-68442-188-6  (hc)
I. Success—Psychological aspects—Quotations, maxims, etc. I. Title.
BF637.S8B25 2003
158.1—dc21
                                                            2003010620

*This book is dedicated to the five most special*
*and influential people in my life:*

Jeanne—my wife and best friend—whose faith
continues to be the richest blessing in my life.
Thanks for showing the way.

Byrd Baggett Jr., the most a son can ask for in a
father. Your passion for life and compassion for
others is a wonderful living legacy. Thanks for
always being there.

Ashley, Amy, and Austin, my true heroes.
I thank God daily for blessing me with such
special, gifted children.

# CONTENTS

* * *

# Acknowledgment

Words can't express the gratitude for Melissa Cook, my multitalented business manager. Thanks for sharing in the vision.

# Introduction

This book is written for those searching for hope; those who have failed and need the encouragement to get up and keep keeping on; those searching for internal peace; those who have been abandoned by so-called friends; those who feel all alone; those who have a vision for the future and need something to lean on; those who need a spark to rekindle the spirit within; those searching for significance; those caught in the "hairball of life"; those searching for wings to their dreams; those searching for the potential hidden within; those searching for something and someone to believe in. If any of the above fits, you will benefit from *The Past Doesn't Have a Future, but YOU Do.*

My vocation (and passion!) as an author and inspirational speaker has allowed me to visit with, and learn from, thousands of successful people from all walks of life—coaches, teachers, professional athletes, clergy, business executives, sales professionals, parents, husbands and wives. This book was conceived when I embarked on a mission to uncover the true essence of a winning lifestyle. To achieve this goal, I sought answers to the question, "What do you consider to be the most important characteristics of winners?" The number-one response came in numerous formats, but focused on the one essential habit required to live a life of success and significance: Don't give up!

The simple goal of *The Past Doesn't Have a Future, but YOU Do* is to share nuggets of inspiration that have proven to help others in their pursuit of hope, passion, and purpose. May the contents touch your heart, energize your spirit and, most importantly, challenge you to take responsibility for your future. May the true riches of life be yours as you *look at life through the windshield, not the rearview mirror.*

# Chapter 1

# THE PAST DOESN'T HAVE A FUTURE, BUT YOU DO

All of life is like a race, with ups and downs and all, and all you have to do to win the race is rise each time you fall. "Quit, give up, you're beaten," they still shout in your face, but a stronger voice inside you says, "Get up and win the race."

—ANONYMOUS

Failure is only absolute when you give up. Everyone gets knocked down; the question is "will you get up?"

⁂

If you don't start, you don't stand a chance of getting there.

⁂

If life is a race, then our purpose is a never-ending finish line.

Successful people do what unsuccessful people won't.

My mother taught me very early to believe I could achieve any accomplishment I wanted to. The first was to walk without braces.

—WILMA RUDOLPH, *three-time Olympic gold medalist, 1960 Summer Olympics*

Adversity tempers the spirit.

---

Your choice: victim or victor.

You must run your own race.
It doesn't matter what other people say
about you. You can do whatever you want
to do as long as it is correct according to
your conscience and your heart.

Failure is temporary; defeat is permanent.

Eighty percent give up after the first try.
Be a twenty-percenter.

I found that I could find the energy,
that I could find the determination
to keep on going. I learned that your mind
can amaze the body if you just
keep telling yourself, "I can do it . . .
I can do it . . . I can do it!"

—JON ERICKSON

The "thrill of victory" often comes right after the "agony of defeat."

Winners focus on "when they will" not "if they can."

The one consistent trait of successful people: they continue to place one foot in front of the other.

Many start, but few finish the race of life.

Individuals *wishing they could*
are certain to be passed by those
*thinking they can.*

There will never be a traffic jam for
those going the extra mile.

We must risk failure to achieve success.

Three steps forward and two steps back
is still progress.

Run *your* race, the race *you* were
born to run.

The difference between a successful person and others is not a lack of strength, not a lack of knowledge, but rather, a lack of will.

—VINCE LOMBARDI

If you believe you are beaten, you are.

---

How do you know that you are having a good day? If you got up on the right side of the dirt!

I dare you to look up at the stars, not down at the mud, and set your sights on a goal that, up to now, you thought was unattainable. There is plenty of room at the top, but no room for anyone to sit down. So, get up, pick the cinders out of your wounds and take one more step. I dare you!

—CLIFF CUSHMAN, *Olympic silver medalist, 1960 Summer Olympics. Killed while defending his country in the Vietnam War, 1966—a true American hero!*

The end is nothing; the road is all.

—Willa Cather

Blessed is the man who perseveres under trial, because when he has stood the test, he will receive the crown of life that God has promised to those who love him.

—James 1:12

Courage leads starward, fear toward death.

—Seneca

Let us run with perseverance
the race marked out for us.

—HEBREWS 12:1

A winner is one who leaves a
legacy of excellence in their chosen
area while giving of themselves to the
betterment of those left behind.

—DR. DAVID COOK

Expect trouble as an inevitable part
of life, and when it comes, hold your
head high, look it squarely in the eye and
say, "I will be bigger than you.
You can not defeat me!"

—ANN LANDERS

Ask not for victory, ask for courage.
For if you can endure you bring honor
to us all, even more you will bring
honor to yourself.

—OLYMPIC MOTTO

We don't lose too often as much
as we quit too soon.

—DAVE WEINBAUM

If you've got the guts to stick it out,
you're going to make it.

—BRIAN HAYS

For every failure, there's an alternative course of action. You just have to find it. When you come to a roadblock, take a detour.

—MARY KAY ASH

If you have made mistakes, even serious
ones, there is always another chance
for you. What we call failure is not the
falling down, but the staying down.

—MARY PICKFORD

Winners choose the playing field
over the sideline.

In the dust of defeat as well as
the laurels of victory, there is glory
to be found if one has done his best.

—ERIC LIDDELL, *1924 Olympic gold
medalist and missionary*

It is impossible to win the race unless you venture to run, impossible to win the victory unless you dare to battle.

—RICHARD DEVOS

Victories often occur after we
see no way to succeed, but refuse
to give up anyway.

—DAVE WEINBAUM

## Chapter 2

# BELIEVE IN YOURSELF AND IN YOUR DREAMS

Doubt sees the obstacles, FAITH sees the way.

Doubt sees the dark of night, FAITH sees the day.

Doubt dreads to take a step, FAITH soars on high.

Doubt questions, "Who believes?"

FAITH answers, "I!"

—ANONYMOUS

Hope is the ability to hear the melody of the future. Faith is the courage to dance to it today.

—ANONYMOUS

The power of the human spirit is beyond measure.

**Happiness Formula:**
Count five blessings before you earn the
right to one worry. Practice this every
morning and every evening for thirty days
and your worries will disappear!

Remember, for all things there is a season.

You don't need an explanation for everything. Recognize that there are such things as miracles, events for which there are no ready explanations. Later knowledge may explain those events quite easily.

—HARRY BROWNE

Make sure you make a daily connection
to the "why" of your life.

He who has a "why" can bear
almost any "how."

—FRIEDRICH NIETZSCHE

**F**aith

**A**lways

**I**s

**T**he

**H**ealing

Life's challenges are no match for the
will of the human spirit.

⁂

One of the worst fates of life is when
hope is replaced by regret.

⁂

Don't let the still, small voice of hope
be drowned out by the loud, angry voice
of despair.

On the street I saw a small girl cold and shivering in a thin dress, with little hope of a decent meal. I became angry and said to God, "Why did you permit this? Why don't you do something about it?" For a while God said nothing.

That night he replied, "I did do something about it, I made you."

The one thing the illness has convinced me of beyond all doubt, more than any experience I've had as an athlete, is that we are much better than we know. We have unrealized capacities that sometimes only emerge in crisis. When you think about it, what other choice is there but to hope? We have two options: Give up or fight like hell!

—LANCE ARMSTRONG,

*Cancer survivor and four-time winner of the prestigious Tour de France*

**The Positive Power of Pain:**
We must persevere through the pain
to get to the promises.

**H**anging

**O**nto

**P**ositive

**E**xpectations

Best way to have hope? Give it.

It has been a wonderful experience to compete in the Olympic games and to bring home a gold medal. But since I have been a young lad, I have had my eyes on a different prize. You see, each one of us is in a greater race than any I have run in Paris, and this race ends when God gives out the medals.

—ERIC LIDDELL, *after winning a gold medal and beginning his life as a missionary. He served as a missionary to China until his death at the age of forty-three.*

Best way to fend off the
"I'm feeling sorry for myself" blues:
Go out and serve someone.

Life has blessed us with the freedom to soar. We must have the **courage** to risk, the **faith** to believe, and the **will** to succeed.

There is comfort among the stars.

# Be a STAR

**S**how

**T**hankfulness

**A**ppreciation

**R**espect

Those who hope in the LORD will renew their strength. They will soar on wings like eagles. They will run and not grow weary. They will walk and not be faint.

—ISAIAH 40:31

All throughout the society,
from the Monarch to the Commoner,
the Spirit was there.

—MARGARET THATCHER *on*
*how the British survived the relentless*
*bombings of World War II*

As a free people, we must
have faith in liberty.

—MARGARET THATCHER

If you have trouble believing in Me,
maybe it will help to know
that I believe in you.

—GEORGE BURNS
*as God in* Oh, God!

Don't quit before the blessing.

Worry is like a rocking chair.
You feel like you're moving, but you
aren't going anywhere.

We shall find peace. We shall hear
the angels. We shall see the sky
sparkling with diamonds.

—ANTON CHEKHOV

**P**ursue

**E**xcellence

**A**nd

**C**herish

**E**very day

More things are wrought by prayer
than this world dreams of.

—ALFRED LORD TENNYSON

Troubles are often the tools by which
God fashions us for better things.

—HENRY WARD BEECHER

Goals are like the stars; they are always
there. Adversity is like the clouds;
it is temporary and will move on.
Keep your eyes on the stars!

Hope is the spark of life.
Share your flame.

# Chapter 3

# MAKE THE MOST OF EVERY DAY

Life is just a minute, only sixty seconds in it.
Forced upon you, can't refuse it,
Didn't seek it, didn't choose it,
But it's up to you to use it.
You must suffer if you lose it,
Give an account if you abuse it.
Just a tiny little minute,
But eternity is in it!

—ANONYMOUS

**L**ive

**I**t

**F**ully

**E**very day

Live each minute as a **Moment of Truth.**
Each minute lived to its fullest is a
**Magic Moment** while each minute wasted
is a **Tragic Moment.**

Every day is a new life to a wise man.

Live life like a two-minute drill.

We only go around once;
make the most of it.

Live like there is no tomorrow.
Learn like you will live forever.

❖

Choose to wear out, not rust out.

I would rather be ashes than dust! I would rather that my spark should burn out in a brilliant blaze than it should be stifled by dry rot. I would rather be a superb meteor, every atom of me in magnificent glow, than a sleepy and permanent planet. The proper function of man is to live, not to exist. I shall not waste my days in trying to prolong them. I shall use my time.

—JACK LONDON

**S**pecial

**M**agic

**I**n

**L**iving

**E**very day

If you fill the unforgiving minute
With sixty seconds' worth of distance run,
Yours is the earth and everything that's in it,
And, which is more, you'll be a man, my son!

—RUDYARD KIPLING

Imagine there is a bank that credits your account each morning with $86,400. It carries over no balance from day to day. Every evening it deletes whatever part of the balance you failed to use during the day. What would you do? Draw out every cent, of course!

Each of us has such a bank. Its name is TIME. Every morning it credits you with 86,400 seconds. Every night it writes off, as lost, whatever of this you have failed to invest to good purpose. It carries over no balance. It allows no overdraft. Each day it opens a new account for you. Each night it burns the remains of the day. If you fail to use the day's deposits, the loss is yours.

There's no going back. There is no drawing against the "tomorrow." You must live in the present on today's deposits. Invest it so as to get from it the utmost in health, happiness, and success. Treasure every moment that you have. Remember that time waits for no one. Yesterday is history. Tomorrow is a mystery. Today is a gift. That's why it's called the *present!*

*A banker friend shared the following:*

Yesterday is a cancelled check; tomorrow is a promissory note; today is cash on hand—spend it!

# Chapter 4

# ACTION WILL TURN YOUR DREAMS INTO SUCCESS

"Come to the edge," he said.

They said, "We are afraid."

"Come to the edge," he said.

They came.

He pushed them . . . and they flew.

—GUILLAUME APOLLINAIRE

Don't get caught in the downdraft
of doubt.

One of the heaviest burdens in life
is great potential.

Failure is either a steppingstone
or tombstone.

The reason so few risk—
the fear of failure.

Great spirits have always encountered violent opposition from mediocre minds.

—ALBERT EINSTEIN

If life were perfect, challenges wouldn't exist. Neither would victories.

Don't wallow in your problem;
rise above it.

If men can reach the moon, you can
reach for the stars.

On the plains of hesitation bleach
the bones of countless millions who,
on the threshold of victory, sat down
to wait, and in waiting, died.

—WILLIAM MOULTON MARSTON

Once you have seen the mountaintop,
you will never be the same.

Winners may fail, but they are
never defeated.

If it can't eat you, don't worry about it.

I am only one, but still I am one.
I may not be able to do everything,
but still I can do something.

—HELEN KELLER

If you're never scared or embarrassed or hurt, it means you never take any chances.

—JULIA SOREL

We must have the courage to bet on our dreams, to take the calculated risk and leave behind forever the internal forces that hold us down.

The two greatest tests of one's character: How one handles adversity and prosperity.

Worry is crabgrass of the soul.

It was of high counsel that I heard given to a young person—"Always do what you are afraid to do."

—RALPH WALDO EMERSON

Be master of your petty annoyances and conserve your energies for the big, worthwhile things. It's not the mountain ahead that wears you out—it's the grain of sand in your shoe.

—ROBERT SERVICE

Courage is resistance to fear, mastery of fear, not absence of fear.

—Mark Twain

Fear is a dark room where negatives are developed.

Three things are extremely hard: steel, a diamond, and to know one's self.

—BENJAMIN FRANKLIN

Nothing changes until the pain of remaining the same becomes greater than the pain of change.

To be a star, you must shine your own light, follow your own path, and not worry about the darkness, for that is when the stars shine brightest.

—ANONYMOUS

Landing and moving about the moon offers so many serious problems for human beings that it will take science another 200 years to lick them.

—*from* SCIENCE DIGEST, 1948

It's not who we are that determines our future, but who we think we are.

---

Fear is nothing more than a mental monster we have created. This monster lives on a daily diet of negative thoughts.

How good can you be? Your best.
How good should you be? Your best.
How good will you be? Your choice!

I can accept failure, but what I can't
accept is not trying.

—MICHAEL JORDAN

Most folks are about as happy as they
make their minds to be.

—ABRAHAM LINCOLN

Turbulence is a necessary part of
the journey.

When confronted with turbulence,
rise above it.

Resign from all your worries. When you can mentally do this, good things have a way of working for you.

Surround yourself with the precious few who believe in you.

Keep your face toward the sun
and you won't see the shadows.

Be an explorer in life.

If an eagle waited for perfect conditions
it would never soar.

Surround yourself with dream makers,
not dream killers.

# A Friend's Prayer

*I don't need your wealth, I need your warmth.*

*I don't need your judgment, I need your forgiveness.*

*I don't need your opinions, I need the truth.*

*I don't need your lessons, I need your laughter.*

*I don't need your personality, I need your purity.*

*I don't need your entertainment, I need your presence.*

*I don't need your knowledge, I need your wisdom.*

*I don't need your recognition, I need your compassion.*

*I don't need your acquaintance, I need your friendship.*

## The PNP of Relationships

Plant the seeds of friendship.

Nourish the seeds by performing random acts of appreciation daily.

Pick the fruits of the relationships.

*Remember, what people think, say, or do (to or about you) has nothing to do with you; it's how they feel about themselves.*

True friends love you for who you are,
not for what you have.

Real friends tell you what you
need to hear, not necessarily what you
want to hear.

To succeed it is necessary to accept the world as it is and rise above it.

—MICHAEL KORDA

Aim for success, not perfection. Remember that fear always lurks behind perfectionism. Confronting your fears and allowing yourself the right to be human can, paradoxically, make you a far happier and more productive person.

—DR. DAVID BURNS

Being a recovering perfectionist, I have adopted as my motto the disclaimer often found on clothes made of raw silk: This garment is made from 100 percent natural fibers. Any irregularity or variation is not to be considered defective. Imperfections enhance the beauty of the product.

—SUE PATTON THOELE

Make sure your self-worth is not determined by your net worth, as you will always be bankrupt.

What we resist persists.

You gain strength, courage, and
confidence by every experience in which
you really stop to look fear in the face.
The danger lies in refusing to face the fear,
in not daring to come to grips with it.
You must make yourself succeed
every time. You must do the thing
you think you can not do.

—ELEANOR ROOSEVELT

The problems of this world cannot possibly be solved by skeptics or cynics whose horizons are limited by the obvious realities. We need men who can dream of things that never were.

—JOHN F. KENNEDY

**Three Greatest Obstacles to Peak Performance:**

1. Negative thoughts.
2. Negative words.
3. Negative people.

*Get rid of them!*

You must pay the price if you
wish to secure the blessing.

—ANDREW JACKSON

Want joy and peace?
Practice compassion, patience, kindness,
goodness, gentleness, faithfulness,
and self-control.

Great way to start your day—
a positive word, a positive thought,
or a positive person.

Show me your friends, and I'll
show you your future.

Eagles don't roost in a sparrow's nest.

## Are Your Relationships Healthy?

1. Do you enjoy being with _____?

2. Do you trust _____?

3. Do you feel comfortable sharing your feelings with _____ without fear of retribution?

4. Does _____ listen without judging or offering advice?

5. Does _____ tell you what you need to hear, not necessarily what you want to hear?

6. Has the relationship with _____ improved the quality of your life?

7. Does _____ drain or energize your spirit?

8. Do you feel better after spending time with _____?

*The above should focus on the ten people with whom you associate most frequently (friends, family members, business associates), as it is a proven fact that the quality of one's life is a direct reflection of the quality of one's relationships. How healthy are your relationships?*

## Set Me Free

If you trust me, set me free.
Don't hold on, let me be.
Hold me, support me, encourage me,
But set me free.
For if you really love me,
You will help me achieve
The beautiful rewards
God planned for me.

The greatest gift of life
Is to have my soul set free,
To be that special person
God meant me to be.
For love is the freedom to see
The beautiful child he crafted in me,
And to live the wonderful life
He created for me.

Love me, but set me free.

*The more we hold onto people and things, the more apt we are to lose them.*

## Why People Control

1. Lack of trust.

2. Lack of confidence.

3. Low self-esteem. "I feel better about me when I control you" attitude.

4. Ego/Arrogance. "I'm better than you" attitude.

5. Perfectionism. "Nobody can do it better than me, so I'll do it myself" attitude. Major reason for burnout.

The weak control, while winners let go.

Only the weak will stay in an
environment of control, resulting in a
culture of mediocrity.

Why Thomas Edison, who was
legally deaf, refused the first hearing aid:
"I don't want others' opinions
to affect my thinking."

Look to others for information,
not decisions.

How can one consent to creep when
one feels an impulse to soar?

—HELEN KELLER

Grab a thistle timidly and it pricks you, grasp it boldly and its spine crumbles.

—WILLIAM HALSEY

The difficult we do immediately; the impossible takes a little longer.

—U.S. ARMY SLOGAN

How can one soar with the eagles when he associates with turkeys?

# Chapter 5

# LOOK AT LIFE THROUGH THE WINDSHIELD, NOT THE REARVIEW MIRROR

He failed in business in '31. He was defeated for a seat in the state legislature in '32. He tried another business in '33—it failed. His fiancée died in '35. He had a nervous breakdown in '36. In '43 he ran for Congress and was defeated. He tried again in '48 and was defeated again. He tried running for the Senate in '55. He lost. The next year he ran for vice president and lost. In '59 he ran for the Senate again and was defeated. Finally, in 1860, Abraham Lincoln was elected the 16th president of the United States.

We will never participate in the
promises of the future
if we allow ourselves to be
held captive by the pain
of the past.

The face in the mirror: best friend or worst enemy. It's your choice.

The grass is always greener over the septic tank.

—ERMA BOMBECK

Focus on what's left, not what's lost.

Positive thoughts don't change the facts,
just the focus.

One of the most tragic things
I know about human nature is that all
of us tend to put off living. We are all
dreaming of some magical rose garden
over the horizon, instead of enjoying
the roses that are blooming outside
our windows today.

—DALE CARNEGIE

Don't give up, give it up!

The sun will come up tomorrow.

—ANNIE

When you were born, you cried and the
world rejoiced. Live your life so
that when you die, the world will cry
but you will rejoice.

Great things usually follow
difficult problems.

The odds are with you if you
keep trying.

—KEITH DEGREEN

Let go of the past and go for the future.
Go confidently in the direction of your
dreams. Live the life you've imagined.

—HENRY DAVID THOREAU

Nobody's problem is ideal. Nobody has things just as he would like them. The thing to do is to make a success with what material I have. It is a sheer waste of time and soul-power to imagine what I would do if things were different.

—DR. FRANK CRANE

Things turn out best for the people who make the best of the way things turn out.

—JOHN WOODEN

Ever wonder why fighter pilots have no rearview mirrors?

You can learn from the past,
but you can never return.

Focus on how you can instead of
why you can't.

**Positive Thinking Exercise:**
Instead of thinking "I have to" (go to the game, recital, work, etc.), think "I get to."

Quit thinking about thinking
about quitting!

Learn from failure. Babe Ruth,
remembered as one of baseball's greatest,
struck out almost twice as many times
as he hit home runs.

All my successes have been
built on my failures.

—BENJAMIN DISRAELI

The apprenticeship of difficulty is
one which the greatest of men have
had to serve.

—SAMUEL SMILES

A constant struggle, a ceaseless battle to
bring success from inhospitable surround-
ings, is the price of all great achievements.

—ORISON SWETT MARDEN

Each player must accept the cards that life deals him or her. But once in hand, one must decide how to play the cards in order to win the game.

—VOLTAIRE

Success in life comes not from holding a good hand, but in playing a poor hand well.

—KENNETH HILDEBRAND

When written in Chinese, the word *crisis* is composed of two characters—one represents danger and the other opportunity.

There are two big forces at work: external and internal. We have very little control over external forces. What really matters is the internal force—How do I respond to those disasters? Over that I have complete control.

—LEO BUSCAGLIA

In the end, we do battle only with ourselves. Once we understand this and focus our energy on what we can do to control our lives, we begin to gain important insights into how life works.

—J. STANLEY JUDD

Courage, it would seem, is nothing less than the power to overcome danger, misfortune, fear, and injustice, while continuing to affirm inwardly that life with all its sorrow is good; that everything is meaningful even if in a sense beyond our understanding—and that there is always tomorrow.

—Dorothy Thompson

The Chinese bamboo plant is a powerful example of perseverance. During the first four years after planting, even though it is watered and fertilized regularly, it grows very little in height. After the fifth year, the plant grows nearly ninety feet in height! The question: Did the Chinese bamboo tree grow ninety feet in five weeks or in five years? The answer is that it grew ninety feet in five years. We are like this amazing plant; we must continue to water and fertilize our life with hope, faith, and perseverance, or we will die and leave our dreams to wither away.

# Chapter 6

# When You Stop Giving, You Stop Living

The loving word you say today,
The thoughtful thing you do,
Will sometime find some special way
Of coming back to you.
The help you gave, you'll see return
Some day when you're in need;
The one to whom you gave your hand
Will be a friend, indeed.
The smile you gave to someone else
Will brighten your own face.
The sunshine that you spread
Will make your world a happier place!

—ANONYMOUS

You can't live a perfect day without doing something for someone who will never be able to repay you.

—JOHN WOODEN

When you stop giving, when you stop offering something, it's time to turn out the lights.

—GEORGE BURNS

## Goal for Today:

Be a blessing in someone's life.

Why worry about the gray hair in the mirror? Think about the cancer patient in chemo who wishes she had hair to examine.

Should you find yourself at a loss and questioning what life is all about, be thankful, for there are those who didn't live long enough to get the opportunity.

How wonderful it is that nobody need to wait a single moment before starting to improve the world.

—ANNE FRANK

Get out of your problems and touch someone's heart.

S pecial

M agic

I n

L oving

E veryone

The only thing that life owes you is a hand up, not a hand out.

These are the times that try men's souls. The summer soldier and the sunshine patriot will, in this crisis, shrink from the service of their country; but he that stands it now, deserves the love and thanks of man and woman.

—THOMAS PAINE

It is from numberless diverse acts of courage and belief that human history is shaped. Each time a man stands up for an ideal, or acts to improve the lot of others, or strikes out against injustice, he sends a tiny ripple of hope, and crossing each other from a million different centers of energy and daring those ripples build a current which can sweep down the mightiest walls of oppression and resistance.

—JOHN F. KENNEDY

All that is necessary for evil to triumph
is for good men to do nothing.

—EDWIN BURKE

Alone, hearts are one of life's most
fragile things, but together their passion can
accomplish the impossible.

Never doubt that a small group of thoughtful, committed people can change the world. Indeed, it is the only thing that ever has.

—MARGARET MEAD

In every community, there is work
to be done. In every nation, there are
wounds to heal. In every heart,
there is power to do it.

—MARIANNE WILLIAMSON

### The Secret to Peace

The fruit of silence is prayer.
The fruit of prayer is faith.
The fruit of faith is love.
The fruit of love is service.
The fruit of service is *peace*.

—MOTHER TERESA

## Chapter 7

# LIVE EACH DAY
# WITH PASSION, AND
# YOU'LL NEVER
# HAVE REGRETS

The life cycle is all backwards. You should die first and get it out of the way. Then you live for twenty years in an old-age home, and get kicked out when you're too young. You get a gold watch and then you go to work. You work forty years until you're young enough to enjoy your retirement. You go to college and you party until you're ready for high school. Then you go to grade school, you become a little kid, you play, you have no responsibilities, you become a little baby . . . and you finish off as a gleam in someone's eye!

—*from* A WHACK ON THE SIDE OF THE HEAD

*by Roger Von Oech*

Follow the trail to your dreams, not the
path of others' expectations.

Listen to the calling of your heart and
the true riches of life will follow.

Happy the man, and happy he alone,
He who can call today his own; He who,
secure within, can say: Tomorrow, do thy
worst, for I have lived today.

—HORACE, *Roman poet*

The two most reliable predictors of success: hope and passion. How are you doing?

How old would you feel if you didn't know how old you were?

—SATCHEL PAIGE

Winston Churchill initiated his protest against Hitler as prime minister at sixty-five. He returned to the House of Commons as a member of Parliament at eighty. When Churchill was interviewed on his eighty-seventh birthday, a young reporter commented, "Sir Winston, I hope to wish you well on your one-hundreth birthday." Churchill quickly replied, "You might do it. You look healthy."

Do you know people who brighten the room when they leave? Avoid them!

Vision is the gift to see what others only dream.

Your vision will become clear
only when you can look into your own
heart. Who looks outside dreams;
who looks inside awakens.

—CARL JUNG

A passionate heart committed to a clear
vision can accomplish the impossible.

Passion is the high-performance
fuel of life.

Some people feel the rain
and some just get wet.

The future belongs to those who
believe in the beauty of their dreams.

—ELEANOR ROOSEVELT

If life doesn't light your fire, you'd better
check your wick.

My life been a good life all my life. I've enjoyed my life. The world don't owe me nothin', not nothin'. A good life is worth living. Writing my name—that was one of the grandest things I learned. . . . I didn't know how to write my name. I wrote X's. That was my name for 100 years, that X. That was all I had.

—GEORGE DAWSON, *who went back to school to learn to read and write—at the age of 98!*

*From his biography,* Life Is So Good.

Count your blessings, not your worries.

There are many things in life that will catch your eye, but only a few will catch your heart . . . pursue those.

Life is no brief candle for me. It is a sort of splendid torch which I have got hold of for the moment, and I want to make it burn as brightly as possible before handing it off to future generations.

—GEORGE BERNARD SHAW

Passion is the spark of life. Without it, life has no meaning.

Years leave wrinkles upon the skin,
but loss of enthusiasm leaves
wrinkles on the soul.

A day without inspiration is like a day
without sunshine.

You don't hear so much about people with a dream today. It's almost as if they're afraid to discover what they're individually capable of and would rather just follow the other fellow. But all of us have more inside us than we believe possible. We have to dream big and dare to fail to bring it out.

—*Explorer* NORMAN VAUGHAN,
*who in 1995, at age 89, was the first person
to scale the 10,302-foot mountain that he
and the legendary explorer Richard Byrd
had discovered sixty-five years earlier.*

Enthusiasm has a way of rolling over
the mistakes.

The grave is a terrible place
to waste potential.

Far too many people tiptoe through life
so they can arrive at death safely.

George Bernard Shaw produced an award-winning play when he was ninety-four years old. Benjamin Franklin helped frame the constitution of the United States when he was eighty-one years old. The fact is, it doesn't matter when you do something great. Age has very little to do with ability.

You're as old as your newest idea.

Do you know people in their twenties who act like they're eighty and people in their eighties who act like they're twenty? Which person are you?

Throw your heart over the fence and
the rest will follow.

—Dr. Norman Vincent Peale

What is required is sight and insight—
then you might add one more: excite!

—Robert Frost

Do your work with your
whole heart and you will succeed—
there's so little competition.

—ELBERT HUBBARD

The only thing that is owed us
is an opportunity of fairness.
The rest is up to us.

Those who do not know how
to weep with their whole heart don't
know how to laugh either.

—GOLDA MEIR

Winners learn from the past, focus on the present, and prepare for the future.

When the sun comes up, you'd better be running.

John Wesley traveled 250,000 miles on horseback, averaging 20 miles a day for 40 years; preached 4,000 sermons; wrote 400 books; and knew 10 languages.  At 83, he was annoyed that he could not write more than 15 hours a day without hurting his eyes, and at 86, he was ashamed that he could not preach more than twice a day. He complained in his diary that there was an increasing tendency to lie in bed until 5:30 in the morning!

**Quote on My Tombstone:**
He died with all of his potential used up.

# Chapter 8

# THOUGHTS FOR
# YOUR JOURNEY

Thoughts without action are simply daydreams.

How long will you falter between
two opinions?

—I Kings 18:21

Change is inevitable, growth is optional.

The winds of change will either blow
you away or take you to new heights.

There is danger in the comfort zone. Are you a victim of comfort?

We will all experience one of the following pains in life: the pain of discipline or the pain of regret. To grow, we must choose the pain of discipline or do nothing and live with the horrible pain of regret. It's your choice.

Insanity is continuing the same habits and expecting different results. What bad habits are you planning to improve upon?

Life doesn't reward what we need but what we deserve.

**Five Steps to Effective Decision Making:**
1. Stop!
2. Ask the right questions from the right people.
3. Listen objectively—with an open mind and heart—to their answers.
4. Think about the consequences of your choices.
5. Respond appropriately.

Fast Action Changes Things

**We Have Four Choices in Life:**

I. The choice of **comfort**. In the transmission c
life, we are in park.

2. The choice of **compromise**. In the transmission of life, we are in reverse.

3. The choice of **confusion**—we know we need
to change but don't know what to do or who to
turn to, so we just stay the same. In the transmission of life, we are stuck in neutral.

4. The choice of **courage**. This is the only choi
that leads to a life full of success *and*
significance. In the transmission of life, this
is overdrive!

*What choice will you make?*

**Want to live a magical life?**
Here's how:

**M**agic

**A**lways

**G**reets

**I**ntensive

**C**ommitment

Take what you got and make
what you got better.

---

Work hard, do your best, live the truth,
trust yourself, have some fun!

*The only one who can take care of you is you.*
How to take the best **CARE** of your life:

**C**hoices you make. There are consequences
to our choices.

**A**ttitude you take. It's either good or bad.

**R**esponsibilities you accept. You get out of
life what you put into it.

**E**xcellence in all thoughts, words, and actions.

**Choose Effectiveness over Activity:**
John Henry Fabre conducted an experiment
with processionary caterpillars, so named
because of their peculiar habit of blindly
following each other no matter how they are
lined up or where they are going. This
researcher took a group of these tiny creatures
and did something interesting with them. He
placed them in a circle, and for twenty-four
hours the caterpillars dutifully followed one
another around and around. He then placed
the caterpillars on a round saucer full of pine
needles (their favorite food). For six days the
mindless creatures moved around and around
the saucer, literally dying of starvation and
exhaustion even though an abundance of choice
food was located less than two inches away.

*Moral of this story: Don't confuse activity
with accomplishment!*

### Six Cs for Effective Daily Living:

1. Competence—learn something new every day.
2. Communication—ask the right questions and you will get the right answers.
3. Compassion—make someone feel appreciated.
4. Character—always do right.
5. Connection—plant the seeds of relationships and nourish them with random acts of appreciation.
6. Commitment—be consistently committed to the above.

You're either green and growing or ripe and rotting. Don't become a victim of comfort!

---

Want to be more creative? Since creativity is most often found in the silence of solitude, we must discipline ourselves to seek it frequently. Do you?

---

The man who does not read good books has no advantage over the man who cannot read at all.

—MARK TWAIN

## Recommended Reading

- *The Power of Positive Thinking,* Norman Vincent Peale
- *Man's Search for Meaning,* Viktor Frankl
- *The Four Agreements,* Don Miguel Ruiz
- *The Alchemist,* Paulo Coelho
- *The Greatest Salesman in the World,* Og Mandino
- *Think and Grow Rich,* Napoleon Hill
- *How to Stop Worrying and Start Living,* Dale Carnegie
- *Acres of Diamonds,* Russell Conwell
- *Soar with Your Strengths,* Donald Clifton
- *Now, Discover Your Strengths,* Marcus Buckingham and Donald Clifton
- *The Lemming Conspiracy: How to Redirect Your Life from Stress to Balance,* Bob McDonald and Don Hutcheson

### 4-Way Test

Take this on a daily basis:

1. Are you competent? Did you learn something new today?
2. Did you listen to your conscience?
3. Is your character sound?
4. Did you have compassion for others today?

## Truly You

There's something out there that you must find,
For what you know, you cannot deny.
Freedom and hope are what you need,
If only you could truly succeed.
All your life you strive to be the best,
But what you really feel, no one could fully
   suppress.
And as you walk onto that stage,
This character, not who you are, is portrayed.
Think of what you really want to be,
And what other people need to see.
Be yourself and be your best,
And don't care about the rest.
Because when it's time to look back at the past,
You want to see the true you,
And how you came to be your best.

—AUSTIN BAGGETT, *age 16, author's son and hero*

## How To Be Your Best

1. Find your seed of greatness.
2. Plant it in your heart.
3. Nourish it with the knowledge and skills necessary to grow to your full potential.
4. Believe in yourself.
5. Focus your energies on positive thoughts, words, and people.
6. Achieve your dreams!

**Greatness Formula:**

*Talents  x  (Knowledge + Skills) = Strengths*

## Less Is More

Worry less, live more.
Do less, achieve more.
Speak less, learn more.

# LET YOUR LIFE SPEAK!